Divorce and Teens

Divorce and Teens

When a Family Splits Apart

Elizabeth Price

Enslow Publishers, Inc.

40 Industrial Road	PO Box 38
Box 398	Aldershot
Berkeley Heights, NJ 07922	Hants GU12 6BP
USA	UK

http://www.enslow.com

Dedication

To my parents who divorced early in my life but always made me feel loved and to my husband, Tom, who inspires me always.

Library of Congress Cataloging-in-Publication Data

Price, Elizabeth.
    Divorce and teens : when a family splits apart / Elizabeth Price.
       v. cm. — (Teen issues)
    Includes bibliographical references and index.
    Contents: Introduction — Dealing with the divorce emotionally — The role of the court in divorce — After the divorce: living a new life—Coping with your parents' new lives — Stepfamilies — Final words.
    ISBN-10: 0-7660-1670-6 (alk. paper)
    1. Divorce—United States—Juvenile literature. 2. Divorced people—United States—Family relationships—Juvenile literature. 3. Children of divorced parents—United States—Psychology—Juvenile literature. 4. Teenagers—United States—Psychology—Juvenile literature. 5. Teenagers—United States—Life skills guides—Juvenile literature. [1. Divorce. 2. Family problems. 3. Stepfamilies.] I. Title. II. Series
    HQ834.P744 2003
    306.89—dc21
                                2003002541
ISBN-13: 978-0-7660-1670-5

Printed in the United States of America

10 9 8 7 6 5 4 3 2

To Our Readers: We have done our best to make sure that all Internet Addresses in this book were active and appropriate when we went to press. However, the author and publisher have no control over and assume no liability for the material available on those Internet sites or on other Web sites they may link to. Any comments or suggestions can be sent by e-mail to comments@enslow.com or to the address on the back cover.

Contents

1

Introduction

lison lived with her mom and dad until she was ten years old. By the time she turned thirteen, her parents were divorced. "When I was little, my dad read me a bedtime story every night. And every one of those stories ended with 'and they lived happily ever after.' I thought that's the way things were supposed to be. What was wrong with my parents?" Alison wondered.[1]

Teens have a lot of company if they have parents who are no longer living together. According to the 2000 U.S. Census, the number of children in new divorces each year is one million. Divorce, once very uncommon, now seems to be an everyday occurrence. Statistics from the 2000 U.S. Census show that more than 50 percent of marriages ended in divorce and over a million divorces occurred in the United States each year.

It might seem to a teen that nothing could be worse than finding out that his or her parents are divorcing. For

For many teenagers, it is heartbreaking when parents separate or divorce.

Alison, it was heartbreaking. "It really did feel like the end of the world. I didn't want to go to school or do anything. I didn't want to talk to anybody. I could hardly think about anything else but the divorce. I will never forget the day my parents sat me down in the kitchen and told me that they were getting a divorce. I just felt empty inside but I couldn't cry about it. Not then, but later I cried under my covers."[2]

Divorce does not have to be the end of the world. It can be the beginning of a changed but, hopefully, new, better, and happier life.

Why Are My Parents Divorcing?

When two people marry they sign papers making their marriage legal. To divorce means to legally end the marriage by judgment or decree of a court.

Couples divorce for many reasons. Some might divorce for personality differences or because they have different visions of how married life should be. Perhaps their needs and common interests have changed. Marriages can also end because of domestic violence, drug, or alcohol abuse, or if one spouse has cheated on the other. Sometimes it is not clear why parents divorce, but whatever the reason, it is *never* the fault of the children. Children should not blame themselves for the divorce.

Divorce is almost always painful for everyone in the family. If there are children involved, divorce is even more complicated. It may mean fights over who gets custody of the children and where and with whom they will live.

Alison still misses seeing her father every day, although she sees him every other weekend and on several days during the week. The divorce has made her life better because it is less tense in her two homes. Alison has made friends in her father's neighborhood. "Some of the changes in my life are an improvement, but I wish my parents were still married."[3]

Parents Fighting With Each Other

"When my parents finally decided to get divorced, I was relieved," says Jennifer, now grown-up, but twelve when her parents divorced. "My parents were always fighting and screaming at each other," she says. "The fights were terrible. At first in the middle of the night I would hear them yelling at each other. I thought they were going to kill each other. Then they started fighting during the days when my sister and I were awake. It was very scary. I used to put a pillow over my head so I wouldn't hear the screaming. Sometimes I used to blame myself, thinking it was something I did. My sister, who was younger than me, didn't seem to care as much as I did about the fights. I used to try and break up the fights."[4]

Seeing parents fight can be very hard on children. For years, Sara, now an adult, blamed herself for her parents' divorce. When she was ten, her mother came home and asked her to clean up her room. She told her mother she would do it later. Her mother told her again to clean her room. Sara's father joined in and said that she could wait to clean the room. Her mother got very angry, and her parents started fighting. Her father hit her mother. Her mother told him that was the final straw; she wanted a divorce. Sara remembers her father crying that day. "I saw myself as the reason my mother wanted the divorce. It took years for me to realize that I was not to blame. My parents' divorce was not caused by me not wanting to clean my room but by a long history of problems that I had nothing to do with."[5] Children need to know that they did not cause their parents' divorce. They also need to understand that the causes of divorce are adults' problems—not theirs.

2

Dealing With the Divorce Emotionally

f I have advice about being a teenager and having your parents divorce, I would say that stability is very important. If kids have a good home and feel loved by both parents, then I think divorce doesn't have to be a negative thing. When my parents divorced, I still felt loved by them and still do to this day.

—Victoria[1]

Why Does One Parent Have to Move Out?

If you have always lived with both of your parents, there is almost nothing worse than having to watch one parent move out. The scene will be on your mind for a long time. Do not be surprised if you find yourself thinking about it often. Trying to pretend that it does not hurt is not a good idea. Learning to cope with the emotions stemming from a divorce is very important. "For kids in separation and divorce, the pain they experience is the loss of the fantasy of perfection or hope that parents' relationship—and their home—can or will get better," says Dr. Syd Brown, a child psychologist.[2]

Amanda and John had to deal with such a situation when their parents separated but were still living in the same house. They knew one of their parents would have to move out, but they did not want either one to leave. Their dad lived in the guest bedroom until the divorce papers were final and the judge said that he had to move out. John remembers the day when he went to answer the doorbell. A man was standing there with some papers for his father. The next day their father moved out.[3]

In most divorce cases, children wish that their parents, who have been able to fix almost anything, could fix their marriage. For many teens, this is the first time they are

Dr. Syd Brown, a psychologist, helps teenagers cope with problems arising when parents divorce.

forced to realize that their parents are human, and not superheroes. Dr. Brown says this happens to a lot of children in divorce. "Kids in separation and divorce situations must come to a wrenching change rather than a gradual change of their boundaries. The boundaries are their home boundaries as two homes are established, not just one, and family boundaries as they are introduced to, and asked to trust, new adults."[4]

Why Are My Parents So Angry With Each Other?

A marriage often ends with anger, bitterness, and hostility, but sometimes two people can just decide a marriage is over and part peacefully. The most important thing for a teen to remember is to try and stay out of the arguments.

Ellen recalls coming home from school one day and finding her parents screaming at each other. Ellen's way of dealing with her parents' fights was to lock herself in her

When your parents divorce . . .

There are some concerns you might have when your parents divorce or separate . . .

What if my dad doesn't come for my brother and my sister on his weekend?
What if mom doesn't have the money to pay the bills?
What if I live with my mom; will my dad be upset or angry?
What if my mom remarries and I don't like him?
What if my dad treats his and his fiancee's children better than my sister and me?

CHILDREN'S BILL OF RIGHTS
WHEN PARENTS ARE NOT TOGETHER

Every kid has rights, particularly when mom and dad are splitting up. Below are some things parents shouldn't forget—and kids shouldn't let them—when the family is in the midst of a break-up.

- **You have the right to love both your parents. You also have the right to be loved by both of them.** That means you shouldn't feel guilty about wanting to see your dad or your mom at any time. It is important for you to have both parents in your life, particularly during difficult times such as a break-up of your parents.

- **You do not have to choose one parent over the other.** If you have an opinion about which parent you want to live with, let it be known. But nobody can force you to make that choice. If your parents can't work it out, a judge may make the decision for them.

- **You're entitled to all the feelings you're having.** Don't be embarrassed by what you're feeling. It is scary when your parents break up, and you're allowed to be scared. Or angry. Or sad. Or whatever.

- **You have the right to be in a safe environment.** This means that nobody is allowed to put you in danger, either physically or emotionally. If one of your parents is hurting you, tell someone—either your other parent or a trusted adult like a teacher.

CHILDREN'S BILL OF RIGHTS continued

- **You don't belong in the middle of your parents' break-up.** Sometimes your parents may get so caught up in their own problems that they forget that you're just a kid, and that you can't handle their adult worries. If they start putting you in the middle of their dispute, remind them that it's their fight, not yours.

- **Grandparents, aunts, uncles and cousins are still part of your life.** Even if you're living with one parent, you can still see relatives on your other parent's side. You'll always be a part of their lives, even if your parents aren't together anymore.

- **You have the right to be a child.** Kids shouldn't worry about adult problems. Concentrate on your schoolwork, your friends, activities, etc. Your mom and dad just need your love. They can handle the rest.

IT IS NOT YOUR FAULT AND DON'T BLAME YOURSELF.

—Special Concerns of Children Committee, March, 1998
American Academy of Matrimonial Lawyers
http://www.aaml.org/billrts.htm 12/5/2003[5]

room. Her sister, Jill, reacted differently to the stress. Jill would beg her parents to stop fighting. She would get in the middle of the fights, and her parents would tell her to leave the room. Then Jill and Ellen's father moved to his own apartment. Jill recalls feeling almost relieved when her father left. The tension was all gone. It was a relief for both of them not to have so much fighting in the house.[6]

In some cases, the tension is resolved or decreased when one parent leaves, but that is not always true. Sam recalls the anger between his parents when his father left. "My mother was so angry at my father that I thought she would do something terrible to him. When my father came to pick us up, she would get into fights with him. It was so awful. My mother took all his stuff and put it out on the street."[7]

What Do I Tell My Friends?

Sometimes it is hard to tell your friends that your parents have separated or divorced. But teens should not feel this way since there were 19.8 million children under 18 in the United States who live with one parent.[8]

Tina remembers feeling very uncomfortable telling her friends that her parents had broken up. "After my mom moved out, I went to school and felt like I [was] living a lie. I remember thinking that so many kids lived with their mothers and that I was the only one who lived with my father. Why did I have to be so different from the other kids?" Later Tina was able to confide to her friends that her parents were not living together anymore. "I found out that almost all the kids were understanding and most thought that it was cool that I was living with my father most of the time."[9]

If others make unkind or even mean remarks, it is very possible that they have their own painful situation. Angela

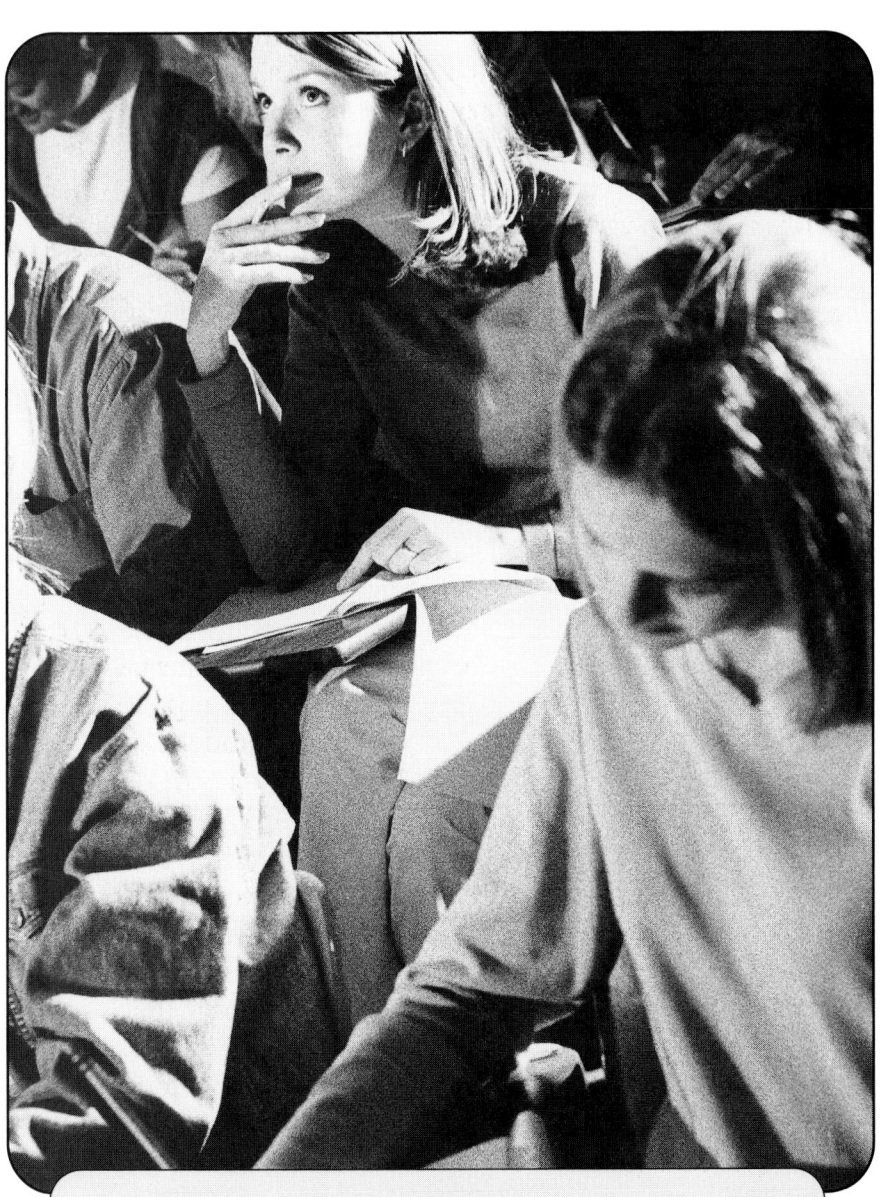

Some teens may be distracted at school when parents are separating or divorcing.

felt horrible every day because a boy in her junior high school made nasty comments about her separated parents. As it turned out, the boy was living with an aunt because both of his parents had abandoned him.[10]

Talking to friends about the divorce might be one thing that you can do. This will allow you to explore your feelings more than by just thinking about them. You might get helpful suggestions from friends in similar situations or from those who have been through it. You may find out how some of them coped with their parents' breakup. You could also be providing them an opportunity to talk about their own feelings.

One Saturday, Nick had to go to his friend's house to work on a term paper. Nick only saw his father on alternate weekends, so this was something of an inconvenience. During the afternoon, he told his friend Arthur how bad he felt having to take time away from his father's visitation. Arthur did not say much at first, but eventually he revealed to Nick that, because of a court order, he was not even allowed to see his own father. Neither of them could change their situation, but both of them felt a little better being able to discuss it openly.[11]

Loyalty to Each Parent

One of the big problems facing teens of divorced parents is divided loyalty. Some teens are torn apart by feeling that they have to decide which parent they like better or which parent they want to live with. This usually happens most often when there is open hostility between the parents. Teens do not have to choose between parents. It is very important to understand that your parents are divorcing each other, not you.

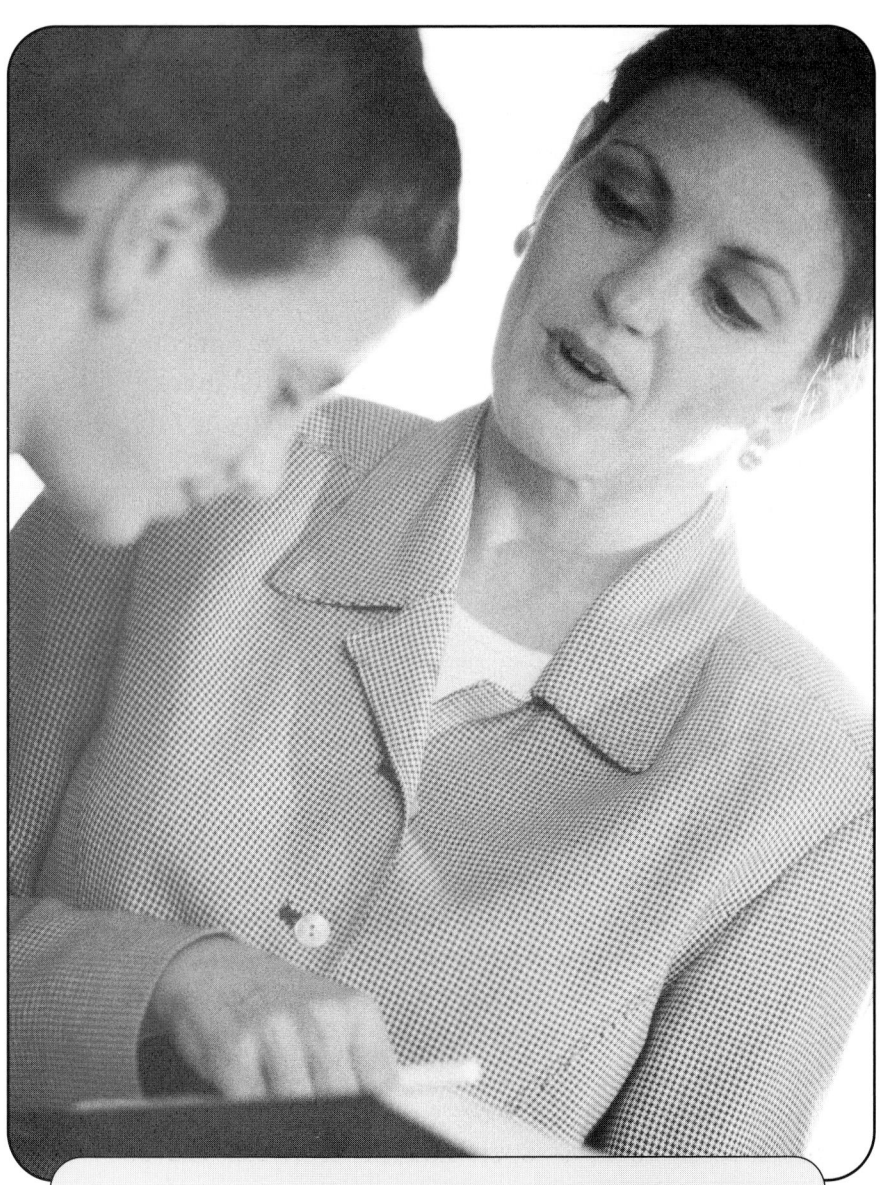

Sometimes it helps to discuss problems with a school counselor or a trusted adult.

"It's imperative that divorcing parents put their children before their legal battles," said Mike McCurley, past president of Academy of Matrimonial Lawyers. "It's important for parents to remember that their actions during divorce have long-term consequences. Children are part-mom and part-dad and need both parents in their lives."[12]

"When my dad took me on a vacation to California after the divorce, I felt really angry at my father," Bobby remembers. "I saw that my mother was home all alone and we were going on this vacation without her. I wanted to have a good time, but I just couldn't on that first vacation. I realize now that I acted really badly toward my father on that trip. I wish I had understood more about why my father left my mother. Now that I am older I think I can understand more."[13]

When Anger Takes Over

Anger is very common in divorces, but it is important for parents not to criticize the other parent in front of their children.

Learning how to cope with your parents' anger toward each other is very important for a teen. Sometimes the anger felt by one parent toward the other lessens over the years, but sometimes it stays the same or gets worse.

Recent court actions in New York State have transferred custody when a parent has interfered with visitation or has told the children negative things about their other parent. Many judges feel it is in the child's best interest to live with a parent who supports a relationship between the children and the other parent and does not try to destroy the other parent's relationship with the child.[14]

Jamie remembers the terrible feeling she had when her mother started saying horrible things about her father. "I love both my parents, and to hear my mother say what a terrible person my father [was] hurt me so much. Her parents, my grandparents, also said the most awful things about my dad. I knew the things they said were not true but it made me uneasy being around my father for a while."[15]

Jamie also says she came to realize that her father was a good person who just was not happy living with her mother. "I now realize the divorce was for the best, but for a while I felt all alone. I missed my father and couldn't stand hearing bad things said about him."

Now that three years have passed, Jamie's mother's anger has cooled down only slightly. She still picks a fight with her ex-husband whenever she can. But Jamie has learned to tell her mother that she does not want to hear bad things about her father and walks away when her mother starts up about her father. "Leaving the room when my mother and grandmother start up about my father is the best thing I can do," says Jamie. "I remember the first time I told my mother I didn't want to hear what she was saying about my father. My mother was shocked. I never had the nerve to do such a thing before, but I couldn't stand it anymore." Jamie thinks her mother has stopped saying bad things about her father in front of her because she put her foot down about bad-mouthing her father.[16]

If a teen is feeling lonely and unsure about how to adjust to his or her parents' divorce, it is best to try to get counseling or at least talk to a friend or another adult about their feelings.

3

The Role of the Court in Divorce

he actual divorce was not as bad as what came before it. I couldn't stand the fighting. The divorce process was peaceful compared to the mess everything was in before my father moved out.

—Victoria[1]

Going to Court

In order to end a marriage, partners must get a divorce decree, which is a piece of paper signed by a judge.[2]

The purpose of a court is to find justice. This means making a legal, fair, and unbiased decision to resolve a matter. A court does that by collecting evidence and hearing testimony. In a divorce, one part of the evidence is called "grounds for divorce." The court also gives legal approval to the decisions made as to whom gets to keep what possessions acquired during the marriage, such as cars, jewelry, houses, money, and sometimes even the family pet.

Most custody and visitation arrangements and schedules are decided and agreed upon between the parents. Judges do not like to tell parents when they can see their children. Judges prefer that the parents agree on their own. The judge reviews everything to ensure the best interests of the children are intact and then orders the divorce decree.

Different States, Different Laws

The United States Constitution allows each state to have its own rules or grounds for a divorce. These rules vary from state to state. If both people want a divorce, getting one from the court is called an uncontested divorce. According to the New York State Unified Court System, an uncontested divorce can only be obtained if (a) there are no disagreements between the spouses over any financial or divorce-related issues (i.e., child custody and support, division of marital property or spousal support); and (b) if each spouse either agrees to the divorce, or fails to appear in the divorce action.[3]

Many states have no-fault divorce, where the only reason required is the desire of both parties to be divorced. No-fault divorce laws allow couples to divorce simply because they do not wish to be married anymore. No one has to accuse the other of doing something wrong.[4]

They can get divorced simply because they have irreconcilable differences which means they just cannot get along and it doesn't look like they will be able to get along.[5]

When One Parent Does Not Want the Divorce

Even if one parent does not want the divorce, it will still happen, the process will just take longer. Sometimes parents cannot agree on how to divide things that they shared when they were married or they cannot agree on custody of their children. Sometimes one parent does not want the divorce at all. In these cases, it is called a contested divorce. Both parents will have to get lawyers, and the court may appoint a law guardian to represent the legal interests of the children, especially if there are any suspicions of neglect or abuse. "I wasn't even nine years old and I had my own lawyer," recalls Nick. "Even though I was pretty upset by the divorce, I felt kind of special."[6]

"First my dad divorced my mom so he could get married to his girlfriend, then, when he got laid off from his job, he took my mom back to court so he could reduce the child support payments. I felt so bad for my parents," said Alison, who was ten when her parents separated. They were still fighting in court when she was thirteen.[7]

Judges are supposed to be impartial decision makers, which means he or she does not take sides. When a judge is satisfied that all the evidence is in order, then he or she will sign a court order and place his or her seal on the order. In an uncontested divorce, the judge usually accepts whatever agreements the parties have made and signs the court order.

Sometimes when a family splits apart, the court will appoint a law guardian to represent the legal interests of the children.

A judge helps parents and children get through the legal process of divorce, unlike the one shown here.

In a contested divorce, a judge will have to make some decisions based on the evidence. The judge might discover some of the evidence from talking directly to the children. This is usually done in the judge's office or chambers.

One other person who might be part of the divorce process is the court-appointed psychologist, psychiatrist or other mental health professional or expert. This person may meet with the couple together and separately, and may also meet with the children, with or without their parents, to assess parent-child relationships, and to identify the conflict areas in the custody-visitation decision-making process. The expert psychologist reports back to the court with recommendations as to whom the children should live with and how much time the children should spend with each parent.[8] It is important for teens to be honest about their feelings about the divorce and their feelings about each parent.

Getting Through the Legal Process of a Divorce

Some states have programs that are designed to help children and teens cope with divorce. New Jersey is one state that has a court-run program called Kids Count. The program allows kids who are going through a divorce a chance to view the courtroom, ask the judge any questions they may have, and express any concerns about the divorce process.[9] This may help to alleviate fears the teen has about the legal process. "Dear Mom," a thirteen-year-old wrote while in the Kids Count program, "I am a little confused on how I feel, but I am happy that you aren't together to fight. I am also sad, though, that you split up."[10] The Kids Count court mediator, Pamela Homan, says, "Some children don't want to take part in the program at first, but once they get involved they tend to get a lot out of the program."[11] Programs like Kids Count help children deal with what might be the puzzle of divorce court. The more information people have, the less anxious and worried they will be. Also, teens get the chance to meet and to interact with other teens in similar situations.

Are There Places I Can Go to Get Help Understanding My Parents' Divorce?

States like Minnesota, Florida, and Delaware have mandatory education programs for children and families going through divorce. Other states are in the process of developing these kinds of programs. In Delaware when a parent files for divorce, custody, and/or visitation, the court requires each parent to attend a class on how to cope with divorce. Each child involved in the divorce must also attend a class on issues raised by the divorce. If both parents do not attend the classes, the judge may question the request for visitation or custody. If one parent does not attend the classes, the judge will weigh that heavily when making a decision on which parent gets custody and how visitation rights are worked out.[12]

Other states offer free and voluntary classes to help parents understand how to help their children get through the divorce. Teens can also attend classes on how to cope with the sometimes confusing issues of divorce.

If a teen understands what the divorce is all about, it makes it easier later on when one parent mentions words such as custody, visitation, or child support. Ask questions, no matter how hard it seems. The more a teen understands, the easier it will be to deal with all the changes caused by the divorce.

Alternative to Divorce Court: Mediation

There is an alternative to going to court and appearing before a judge. Sometimes parents will hire a divorce mediator to work out the major and minor concerns in a divorce. Some states have mandatory mediation programs that parents must attend before they get to see a judge. Mediation is a way of resolving disputes between people without going to court, and it is confidential. Mediation is pro-family and future-focused. The emphasis is on the co-parenting of the children, even though the marriage bond no longer exists. Mediation can be less costly and much healthier for everyone involved than two lawyers arguing in court. However, both parents must agree to participate in mediation before it can happen. Mediation usually consists of both parents meeting with the mediator and discussing such issues as custody and visitation schedules as well as division of property. If both parents agree, then a written agreement will be submitted to the judge. The judge will sign the agreement. The agreement then becomes an order of the court and the parents can be officially divorced.

4

After the Divorce: Living a New Life

The divorce is over. A teen's parents are no longer married. One of the parents is not living in the house, or a teen may have moved with one parent to a new home.

Fifteen-year-old Karen thinks of the first time her father picked her up after the divorce. She remembers being very nervous and thinking maybe he would not come. He did show up, and after a while Karen got used to seeing her father in his new place. "At first I stayed in the house, kind of was scared of the neighborhood, but then I went outside and started meeting other kids. It began to be fun to go over to my father's. I got to be with my father and also had friends I could hang out with. Now that I am in high school I go directly to my father's house after school instead of coming back to my mom's house. I know my mom doesn't like this, but I feel I need to make my own decisions."[1]

Karen is not alone in wanting to make her own decisions

about where she lives. A large percentage of teens feel the need to decide where they want to live. Many state courts allow a teen to choose which parent he or she wants to live with. In California, a teen's living preference is seriously considered. If the judge finds that a teen is mature enough to decide, and the reasons for changing custody are valid, then the teen's preference will be given a lot of weight. Many states have similar rules.[2]

Living With One Parent

Divorce sometimes means that a teen will live with one parent most of the time and spend alternating weekends with the other parent.

When Nicole was in seventh grade, she found it very annoying to have more than one home. "Friends would ask me for my phone number and I wouldn't know what to say. Depending on what day they called me I would have a different number." Using the telephone had not been so important before then. Some teens might find it easier just to tell their friends what number they can be reached at that weekend.[3]

Another issue with Nicole was bathroom supplies. "In my mom's house I had everything I needed. All my dad had was soap, toothpaste, and a bottle of cheap shampoo. I needed my shampoo, conditioner, hair spray, razors, skin cream, and all the other things girls need." She explained to her father that these were necessities, and they went shopping together. "He was completely shocked at how much money all these things cost, but I think he also felt kind of good that he was doing something with me."[4]

In the years following a divorce, one parent may be required to relocate because of their job or because of their new spouse's job. A teen may have to travel great distances to spend time with that parent. Some teens even have to fly to the state where that parent now lives.

Joint Custody

Seventeen-year-old Brian's parents divorced when he was three. He does not remember a time when he lived with both his parents. The court gave his parents joint custody of Brian and his sister; they spend one week at their mother's house and the next week with their father. Vacations are divided, as are summers. Brian likes this arrangement. He has two homes, but since his parents live close together, he goes to the same school no matter which parent he is living with. He knows it was hard at first because his older sister remembers adjusting to living in two houses, but he has never known another way of living. "I sometimes wonder whether my parents like it this way. They get a week off from having to deal with teenagers," says Brian.[5] Other arrangements under joint custody include one month on and one month off or splitting the week between both parents.

Visiting the Other Parent

The custody arrangement that Brian's parents have is not always common; sometimes one parent gets sole custody, and the other parent has visitation rights. Jessie's parents had a difficult divorce when he was ten. The judge felt that his parents could not work together with a joint custody arrangement. There was just too much anger. The court gave Jessie's mother custody, and his father got to see him every other weekend. His mother had the right to make all decisions about his upbringing; however, she had to consult his father on major issues like health care and schools. When Jessie started visiting his father, it was

Visitation sometimes means adjusting to going back and forth between two houses.

tough for him. "I loved my father and wanted to see him all the time."[6]

Joint Custody Alternatives

Some teens have other custody arrangements. Teens sometimes stay with one parent during school and the other on weekends and vacations. Another plan could be a month in one home and the next month in the other. Sometimes it can even be worked out so that the teen stays in the original home and the parents switch residences. One such arrangement happened in British Columbia, Canada, by arranging to let the kids continue to live in the family home while the parents alternate living in the house. The mother stays in the house for three weeks a month, while the father gets the last week of the month. The judge in this divorce felt the children should have stability, and having the parents share the house was the best way to achieve this.[7]

What If I Am Not Happy With the Visitation Schedule?

Living with one parent and "visiting" the other parent is not easy. If a teen is not happy with the custody/visitation schedule, the teen should try talking to his or her parents. The schedule has to be practical. Parents often have obligations that must be met, and that can affect schedules. Parents may disagree on the amount of visitation time. This can become a source of conflict between the parents. A teen might want to talk to a school guidance counselor about this matter. Talking to a counselor might help the teen come to some kind of resolution about the visitation schedule.

5

Coping With Your Parents' New Lives

New Relationships—Parents and Dating

Many teenagers have negative reactions when their divorced parents start dating. It can be a confusing time for parents and children.

"I saw my mother kissing this guy and I was shocked. It seemed so strange to see my mother acting like a teenager," says sixteen-year-old Alice. "I got into a fight with her, telling her that she better grow up and stop acting like a teenager and that if she could act that way I could, too."[1]

According to the 2000 U.S. Census, 43 percent of remarriages were for at least one partner. Teens with divorced parents will most likely have to go through the experience of watching their parents go out on dates and fall in love.

When Alice tried expressing her feelings to other relatives, it only made things more confusing for her. She complained to her grandmother that her mother was acting "immature" with her new boyfriend, Paul. Her grandmother responded that Paul was more easygoing than Alice's father. She compared Paul's willingness to let the whole family stay out late to her father's strict "in bed by ten" attitude.[2]

Alice was upset by the way her mother was behaving, not by the kind of person that Paul was. Even if her parents were divorced, Alice felt that they should not be allowed to be in love with someone else. From Alice's point of view, Paul was a nice guy, but that did not mean that her mother had to have romantic feelings for him.

Not all teens get into arguments with their parents; sometimes they are just shocked or feel hurt. For years after his parents split up, twelve-year-old Eddie was used to hearing his mom call him "sweetheart." Then one day, his mother's boyfriend was having supper at their house. He heard her say, "Sweetheart, could you get me a glass of water?" and was astonished when he realized that she was not talking to him.[3]

Eddie had never heard his mother call anyone else by that name. At first he was embarrassed. He hoped that no one else in the room noticed that he had begun to stand up, and then nonchalantly sit back down, as his mother's boyfriend handled her request. Later, he felt jealous and angry that someone else was given his personal nickname. Since he was not about to tell anyone that his mother still called him sweetheart, he just tried to forget about it.

Watching your parents go out on dates is never easy. Jill remembers when her mother started dating Jim, now her stepfather. "I hated him from the first moment I saw him. He seemed so unlike my father. My sister and I started to laugh the first time he came into the house. He was so funny looking. I don't think he liked us very much either."[4]

Now an adult, Jill can see that she gave Jim a very hard time because she was jealous because she felt someone was trying to replace her father. "I was absolutely awful to him. But he didn't know how to handle me so we fought all the time."[5]

If a teen is hoping that his parents will get back together; dating does not help much. "Divorce is a wrenching pain for teenagers, and when your parents start dating, the pain can get even worse," says Dr. Syd Brown. "First you had to deal with the initial shock of the divorce, and now you have to deal with a new person in your parent's life."[6]

"Seeing my mother hanging out with a new guy made me very angry. I wanted my father back in the house," says fourteen-year-old Elana. "Then my father got a girlfriend and things got worse. I wanted nothing to do with her. I would make fun of her and call her names. When they broke up, I was happy, but I knew my father was very sad." Elana dealt better with the next woman in her father's life. "I knew by the second girlfriend that my father needed love and companionship in his life so I was more accepting of Judith." Elana's father eventually married Judith, and Elana gets along well with her stepmother. Still, it is never easy to watch your parents go out on dates.[7]

Most teens feel loyal to their parents and not to their parents' new partners. Teens may feel guilty if they like their parent's partner. Matt recalls liking his new stepmother but not being able to accept her because he felt he was being disloyal to his mother. His mother fueled these conflicting emotions by often telling Matt how much his father had hurt her when he asked for a divorce.[8]

New Names

Many women change their last names when they remarry. This can put a teen in the position of having a different last

Most teens feel loyal to their parents and not to their parents' new partners.

name from his or her mother. Some teens find this very uncomfortable, especially when uninformed adults confuse the names.

"I hated it every time my mother would meet one of my teachers," recalls Eddie. "They'd call her by my last name and then she had to make a big deal out of telling them what her last name was. She was supposed to be talking about my schoolwork and instead she was bringing this up."[9]

Angela would occasionally be called by her stepfather's last name. "I didn't like him and I was furious with my mom for marrying him. Whenever I heard neighbors or people from his job put my name and his together, I'd have a fit. I'd fantasize that my dad would magically appear and set them straight as to what my name was."[10]

Considering that there are millions of children with different last names from their mothers, it seems that adults would know better. One problem is that many adults do not understand the importance of "getting the name right." Realizing that adults can make mistakes and that there are so many other children in the same predicament can make life a little bit easier.

What Happens on Holidays and Vacations?

Karen remembers that first Christmas after the divorce. "My mother was to have me and my sister on Christmas Eve and on Christmas Day until noon. Then my father was to pick us up and take us on vacation. I didn't want to go with my father. I wanted to stay at home the way we had always done with my mom and dad on Christmas." Karen remembers the fit she had. "I remember my mother telling me that it wouldn't always be like this, that when I was older I could decide what I wanted to do on the holidays.

Code of Etiquette for Children of Divorce

- Don't play one parent off against the other. ("Daddy doesn't mind if I stay out till two in the morning, so I don't know why you do.")
- Treat your parents' new romantic interests with the same courtesy you extend toward all guests.
- Don't assume that your parents' dates wish to steal your mom or dad's affections from you.
- Don't ask your parents for details of what they do on or with dates.
- Never brag about one parent's "new friend" to the other parent. ("He's so cool, Dad. He drives a Ferrari and he said he's teaching me to fly his helicopter.")
- Put yourself in your parents' shoes. They, too, may feel angry, confused, scared, lonely, and betrayed. Try to help each other rather than hurt each other.
- Give stepparents a break. It's as hard for them as it is for you.
- Don't get caught in the middle of your parents' arguments. As you leave the room, say "I love you both and I'm not going to take sides."[11]

So I went, but I made life miserable on that trip. I refused to talk to anybody. The next year my dad traded Christmas Day for an extra day during vacation, which made it easier on everybody. Still I missed seeing my dad on Christmas."[12]

Dividing up holidays and vacations is one of the most difficult parts of the divorce process. The more flexible the parents are about the schedule, the easier it can be for everybody. The court order was very specific that Karen's dad would get his children at 12:00 noon every Christmas.

The visitation schedules that are worked out at the time of the divorce might not be able to stand the test of time. It is common for a judge to advise the parents that teenage children will want to make some changes to accommodate their growing social and educational demands. No one, however, can force either parent to change the visitation schedule without a new decision by a judge.

Karen recalls the time she mentioned changing the visitation schedule to her mother, who had custody. "My mother blew up with anger. All I was doing was asking that I spend more time at my dad's house and stay over on some holidays when he didn't have me. My mother said she wasn't ready to lose me to my father. I still can't believe she said that. I kind of gave up after that, but as soon as I am seventeen I am going to go live with my dad."[13]

Sometimes one of the parents wants to modify the visitation schedule. If the parent changes jobs, goes back to school, or moves, he or she may not be able to adhere to the original schedule. Occasionally, the parent may have strong personal reasons for requesting a change.

Sherri, now an adult, remembers when she was fourteen that her mother asked her to alter the visitation schedule. Sherri spent every Sunday and alternate weekends at her father's. Several years after the divorce, her mother began dating and saw her new boyfriend almost every Saturday.

Dividing up holidays and vacations is one of the most difficult parts of the divorce process.

She asked Sherri to switch to Saturday visitation with her father, so that Sherri could see her on Sundays.[14]

Sherri refused outright. "I remember being so hurt that my mother wanted to change a schedule that had been in place for years so it would make it easier for her to see her boyfriend. I know now that my mother was trying to be reasonable, but at the time I thought it was horrible of her to suggest this. We kept to the Sunday schedule until I went to college."[15]

If a teen is having problems with the visitation schedule, the teen should bring it up to his or her parents. The visitation schedule can be modified if both parents agree. If neither parent seems approachable, a responsible adult, such as a guidance counselor, can be consulted. The visitation schedule is constructed to ensure that the children are well cared for, and it is common for a teen's parents to disagree on what this means.

6

Stepfamilies

When parents remarry, it can be very upsetting to teenagers. It might seem like the final step of the divorce process. Many teens will have fears that they will not belong anywhere if their parents remarry.

In addition to a mom and a dad, most teens have brothers, sisters, grandparents, aunts, uncles, and cousins. If one parent gets remarried, suddenly a teen acquires a large series of steprelatives. If both parents remarry, this effect is doubled. Consider all of the steprelatives that will get divorced and marry other divorced people.

One day a dentist saw two teenage boys joking around in his waiting room. He asked if they were friends or relatives. "He's almost my cousin," said one of them. The dentist smiled and said, "How could that be?" The boy thoughtfully replied, "As soon as his dad marries my stepmother's sister, we'll be cousins." The dentist scratched his head and walked back into his examination room.[1]

One problem with having a variety of steprelatives is what to call them. When Eddie was thirteen, his mother remarried, and he was not sure how to refer to his stepfather's mother. "I felt too weird calling her 'grandma' and didn't even know if she'd want me calling her that. She wasn't that crazy about my mother, so why would she want her little brat implying we were related? But calling her by her first name was really strange. She was sixty years old. I didn't call anybody that old by their first name. I did everything I could to avoid using her name at all."[2]

Eddie discovered that there were some steprelatives that he felt very comfortable with, and he had no problem calling them "aunt" or "uncle."

"My stepfather had this old uncle who seemed to like everybody. He'd sit around and watch TV with me and never asked me anything stupid, like 'What do you want to be when you grow up?' He'd just talk about whatever was on TV. It didn't take me long to start calling him Uncle Chet."

Not every new steprelative made Eddie feel as comfortable. Although his mother and stepfather encouraged him to call step-relatives "aunt" or "uncle," he did not always feel natural about saying it. Eventually, Eddie would refer to some of them with just their first names.[3]

Dealing With Stepparents

After a divorce, teens can find themselves with a new family after one or both of the teen's parents remarry. Stepparents get bad press. A stepfamily can include a stepmother or stepfather, stepbrothers, stepsisters, and possibly half brothers and half sisters. It can even include an added set of grandparents, uncles, aunts, and cousins.

Becoming part of a stepfamily changes a teen's world. Dr. Syd Brown believes that boundaries define people. He says, "In separation/divorce the two adults cannot rely on each other for assistance in boundary definition and maintenance. This demands that the adults reestablish boundaries for themselves and their kids. And also puts additional burdens on kids to set boundaries for themselves and their younger siblings, often before they are ready to do so."[4]

Karen, who is now fifteen, was devastated when her father remarried as soon as her parents' divorce was final.

A stepfamily can include a stepmother or stepfather, stepsisters, stepbrothers, and possibly half brothers and half sisters. It can even include an added set of grandparents, uncles, aunts, and cousins.

Karen felt very hostile toward her dad and new stepmother. "My dad married a woman he had known before he met my mother," she says. "I saw my mother all alone and my father seemed happy, and I just boiled up inside with anger. Now my mother has a boyfriend whom she likes a lot. Things worked out in the end, but for a while I hated my dad for marrying someone else so soon after the divorce. I guess I wanted him to suffer more for ending his marriage with my mother."[5]

Karen hated her stepmother when she first met her. She even made up names to call her. Reflecting on her behavior a couple of years later, she realizes that her stepmother was not an evil person but someone who had inherited kids who were not hers and who were very difficult to deal with.[6]

Alice was ten when she first met her stepmother. She remembers telling her, " 'You stole my father away from my mother and I hate you.' I think I hurt her feelings. I thought if I acted horrible she would go away and my parents would get back together again. I didn't realize that she was not the cause of the problems between my parents." Alice still does not have good feelings about her stepmother, but she has adjusted to her new life.[7]

Another problem facing teenagers who become part of a stepfamily is how to handle feeling affection for the new stepparent without feeling disloyal to their parents.[8] Twelve-year-old Elise does not remember living with both parents. Her parents divorced when she was three, and both remarried within a year of the divorce. Elise remembers her older brother and sister telling her that she should not like her stepmother, Joanna, because their mom did not like her. But Elise remembers always liking Joanna. Her stepmother played with her and, later on, when Elise was older, taught her how to ride a bike and roller-skate. Elise

Learning to live with a stepparent can be difficult, but also fun and rewarding.

remembers feeling strange when other kids would call her stepmother her mom. "I did not understand why other kids would say, 'Your mom is here to pick you up,' when it was my stepmom. I guess I was offended at first, but now I feel I do have two moms. One is the mom who gave birth to me, and the other mom is my friend who loves me a great deal even if I am not her real kid."[9]

Some teenagers like their stepparents. Other teens feel hostility and anger toward the person who "replaced" their father or mother. Beth remembers that as a teen she hated her stepfather. "He didn't want me there and always made it clear that he would rather be alone with my mother. I remember once I came home from school and my mother hadn't gotten home yet. He came into the living room and started yelling at me to start dinner. I refused. He didn't talk to me for a long time." Sometimes the relationship between a teen and a stepparent will be strong and loving. Other times it just will not work. But the important thing is to have mutual respect for each other.[10]

Having Stepsiblings

Learning to live with a stepparent can be difficult enough, but when the stepparent has children of his or her own, new issues come up. Sometimes there is jealousy between the children and resentment of having to share their parent's affection. The situation can sometimes be awkward and uncomfortable, but over time, having stepbrothers or stepsisters can be fun and rewarding.

It is impossible to tell how a person's relationship with his or her stepsiblings will turn out. Maxine Rosenberg wrote in her book, *Talking About Stepfamilies:* "I see that my life has been enhanced since my father's remarriage. Only yesterday, on the telephone, one of my stepsister's and I exchanged news of our joys and difficulties. We confided in each other as if we were biological sisters." [11]

For Eddie, having a brand-new older stepbrother was troublesome. "He didn't live with us, but on the weekends, holidays, and vacations, when he stayed with his father it was very tense. He wanted to make sure that I knew that he was older, stronger, smarter, and better looking. That meant beating me up, showing off his grades, and flaunting all of his girlfriends in front of me. He was already in college, so I didn't feel like we had much in common, but he sure made his point that I wasn't going to replace him."[12]

Eddie was much happier with his new collection of stepcousins. "All of a sudden I had a bunch of kids my age to hang out with. Some of the girls gave me a lot of attention, which was great. I actually found myself asking my mom when we could visit them again."[13]

Jessica's parents divorced when she was eight. By the time she was twelve, she was part of two new families. Her mother married Joe, who shared custody of his two small children. Her father married Kathy, who had three teenage daughters. At first it was hard for Jessica to share her parents with her stepbrothers and stepsisters. Jessica says, "I didn't like sharing a room when I was over at my father's. I shared a room with Angie, my stepsister, who is my age. It was very uncomfortable, but Angie is great and made me feel wanted. We are friends now."[14]

Jessica also remembers not liking her two stepbrothers at first. "They were little and everybody paid attention to them. I had to go places with them. I even had to baby-sit them sometimes," she says. "But now that I am older I see the good points of my mom and dad remarrying. I still have my grandparents, but I also have stepgrandparents who I love a lot. It was hard at first because I didn't know what to call people in my stepfamily, but it works out when I call them by their first names."[15]

It might take awhile to get used to having a stepfamily. In the beginning, it might seem like the worst possible thing that could happen has happened. Learning to live with an adult who is not your parent but who lives with your mom or dad is hard enough. On top of this, having stepbrothers or stepsisters close to your age adds another dimension.

The Arrival of a Half Sister or Half Brother

Sometimes parents who remarry start a family with the new spouse. A teen can have even more doubts about his or her place in the world when a baby is born. Many teens react to the birth of a new half sister or half brother with fear. A teen might be afraid of losing the love of their parent to a new baby.

Kirk felt pangs of jealousy when his mom and stepfather had a baby. "I was twelve when Ashley was born, so I was more like a father to her as she grew up. I got used to her, but it took me a long time to get over my resentment that there was a new baby in the house and that I wasn't the center of attention anymore."[16]

Alison has never really gotten used to having a stepmother, stepgrandparents, and other steprelatives, but over the years it has become easier to deal with the different members of her stepfamily. "I still feel uncomfortable when my stepgrandparents come over to visit. I really don't know what to say to them, but I am polite and try to handle the situation as best as I can. Most of the time I wish my parents were back together and things were like the way they were before the divorce."[17]

Many families today are made up of members from other family groups. You might live with your mother and her new husband or with your father and stepmother. You might have stepbrothers and stepsisters or half siblings. Whatever combination makes up your family, it is part of your world.

7

Final Words

divorce may always cause problems and complications for children. Witnessing the breakup of your parents' marriage—the couple that was supposed to "live happily ever after"—is heartbreaking. One of the parents will move out, and everyone will have to follow visitation schedules. Often there will be financial difficulties. There is a good chance that one of the parents will get remarried and the children will have to deal with a stepfamily.

Divorce can have an impact on a teen's life in different ways. "For some teens, the pain can't be washed away although some parents tell their teenage children things are better now but for some teens the pain continues," comments Dr. Brown.[1]

Some teens survive the turmoil and change better than others. If you are having a difficult time dealing with the divorce, it is best to get help. First, try to talk to your parents, and then, if you still need help or advice, try to find

Find ways to discuss your feelings with the adults in your life.

someone you trust, such as a teacher or a counselor. Craig Henry Leibel, whose parents divorced when he was fifteen, wrote in *Divorce Magazine:* "To let go of the pain and the hurt, it is essential for children of divorce to talk about their feelings with their parents. Divorce is a breeding ground for a lack of communication." He also writes: "We need to ask the hard questions as well as the stupid or ridiculous questions. We need to confront our fears. We need to feel supported and we need to feel loved."[2]

Everybody who goes through the turmoil of divorce deals with it differently, but the most important thing to remember is not to keep feelings bottled up inside. Find ways to discuss your feelings with adults and other teens you trust. Lots of people have felt the same way you do, and it could help you to discuss the good and bad feelings you have about your parents. Lastly, remember your parents are only human. Their mistakes are not yours, and the divorce is not your fault. They divorced each other—not you. You will always be their child.

Chapter Notes

Chapter 1. Introduction
1. Personal interview with Alison, July, 2001.
2. Ibid.
3. Personal interview with Alison, July, 2001.
4. Personal interview with Jennifer, April, 2001.
5. Personal interview with Sara, January, 2002.

Chapter 2. Dealing With the Divorce Emotionally
1. Personal interview with Victoria, January, 2002.
2. Personal interview with Syd Brown, Ph.D., November, 2002.
3. Personal interview with Amanda and John, January, 2002.
4. Personal interview with Syd Brown, Ph.D., November, 2002.
5. "Children's Bill of Rights: When Parents Are Not Together," Special Concerns of Children Committee, American Academy of Matrimonial Lawyers, March, 1998 <http://www.aaml.org/billrts.htm> (December 5, 2003).
6. Personal interview with Jill and Ellen, April, 2001.
7. Personal interview with Sam, April, 2002.
8. "Two Married Parents the Norm," U.S. Census Bureau, *United States Department of Commerce News*, June, 12, 2003, <http://www.census.gov/PressRelease/www/2003/cb03-97.html> (December 8, 2003).
9. Personal interview with Tina, April, 2001.
10. Personal interview with Angela, September, 2001.
11. Personal interview with Nick, July, 2001.
12. Personal interview with Bobby, May, 2001.

13. "Stupid Parent Tricks," *Divorce Magazine*, <http://www.divorcemagazine.com/library/children/stupidparent.html> (December 5, 2003).

14. *New York Law Journal*, Case 183 AD 2d 903.

15. Interview with Jamie, October, 2001.

16. Ibid.

Chapter 3. The Role of the Court in Divorce

1. Personal interview with Victoria, April, 2002.

2. Robert Coulson, *Fighting Fair* (New York: The Free Press, 1983), p. 82.

3. "Divorce: What Is An Uncontested Divorce?," New York State Unified Court System, n.d. <http://www.nycourts.gov/litigants/divorce/index.shtml> (December 5, 2003).

4. "Divorce: An Overview," The Legal Information Institute of Cornell University, n.d. <http://www4.law.cornell.edu/cgi-bin> (December 5, 2003).

5. Constance R. Ahrons, Ph.D, *The Good Divorce* (New York: HarperCollins Publishers, 1994) p. 185.

6. Personal interview with Nick, July, 2001.

7. Personal interview with Alison, July, 2001.

8. "Parental Information," *Psychology Information Online*, n.d., <http://www.psychlogyinfo.com/forensic/mediation.html> (December 8, 2003).

9. *Kids Count Newsletter*, vol. 1, no. 2 September 1999, <http://kidscountprogram.org/newsletter/sept99/index.html> (December 8, 2003).

10. Ibid.

11. Ibid.

12. "Education For Separating and Divorcing Parents," n.d.,<http://courts.state.de.us/family/FAQ_Placeholder/faq/English_Placeholder/education/education/education.htm/> (December 5, 2003).

13. Lori Godin, LMFT, "What is Child Custody Mediation," Change and Renewal <http://www.modernlife. org/all_staples1999to2000/2000Archive/Jan_2K_original/ custodymediation.htm> (January 29, 2004).

Chapter 4. After the Divorce: Living a New Life

1. Personal interview with Karen, September, 2001.

2. Glen L. Rabenn, "Will the Judge Consider the Child's Preference?" Certified Family Law Specialist, CaliforniaDivorce.com n.d. <http://californiadivorce.com/ articles/childspreference.htm> (December 8, 2003).

3. Personal interview with Nicole, July, 2001.

4. Ibid.

5. Personal interview with Brian, July, 2001.

6. Personal interview with Jessie, July, 2001.

7. Jeffrey Cottrill, "Family Home Goes to the Children," *Divorce Magazine*, October 8, 2000 <http://www. divorcemagazine.com/news/100200.shtml> (December 8, 2003).

Chapter 5. Coping With Your Parents New Lives

1. Personal interview with Alice, July, 2001.

2. Personal interview with Alice, July, 2001.

3. Personal interview with Eddie, June, 2001.

4. Personal interview with Jill, April, 2001.

5. Ibid.

6. Personal interview with Syd Brown, Ph.D., November, 2001.

7. Personal interview with Elana, April, 2001.

8. Personal interview with Matt, July, 2001.

9. Personal interview with Eddie, June, 2001.

10. Personal interview with Angela, September, 2001.

11. Excerpted from *How Rude! The Teenagers' Guide to Good Manners, Proper Behavior, and Not Grossing People Out* by Alex J. Packer, Ph.D. © 1997. Used with permission from Free Spirit Publishing Inc., Minneapolis, MN 1-800-735-7323; www. freespirit.com. All rights reserved.

12. Personal interview with Karen, September, 2001.

13. Personal interview with Karen, April, 2001.

14. Personal interview with Sherri, April, 2001.

15. Ibid.

Chapter 6. Stepfamilies

1. Personal interview with Peter, July, 2001.

2. Personal interview with Eddie, June, 2001.

3. Ibid.

4. Personal interview with Syd Brown, Ph.D., November, 2001.

5. Personal interview with Karen, July, 2001.

6. Ibid.

7. Personal interview with Alice, July, 2001.

8. Maxine Rosenberg, *Talking About Stepfamilies* (New York: Bradbury Press, 1990), p. 5.

9. Personal interview with Elise, April, 2001.

10. Personal interview with Beth, April, 2001.

11. Rosenberg, p. 3.

12. Personal interview with Eddie, June, 2001.

13. Ibid.

14. Personal interview with Jessica, October, 2001.

15. Ibid.

16. Personal interview with Kirk, June, 2001.

17. Personal interview with Alison, September, 2001.

Chapter 7. Final Words

1. Personal interview with Syd Brown, Ph.D., November, 2002.

2. Craig Henry Leibel, *Divorce Magazine*, <http://www.divorcemag.com/cgi-bin> (May 23, 2002).

Glossary

child custody—A court order stating which parent minor children live with most of the time.

child support—The amount of money the noncustodial parent pays to the parent who has custody, to help take care of the children.

contested divorce—A divorce where one party does not want the divorce.

divorce attorney—A lawyer specially trained to help people get divorced.

divorce mediation—A process where the two people getting a divorce meet and work out an agreement with a trained mediator. Mediation is an alternative to lawyers and fighting in court. A mediator, like an attorney, helps people to divorce.

divorce—The legal process that ends a marriage.

half brother or half sister—A child who has one parent in common and one different parent.

joint custody—A court order stating both parents share decision making about the children's lives and that the children share almost equal time with each parent.

judge—A court official who presides over a divorce and signs the final court papers making the divorce final.

law guardian—A lawyer appointed to look after the children's interest in a divorce. The law guardian will meet with all parties involved in the divorce, including the children, and make recommendations to the judge about custody and visitation schedules.

legal separation—A written agreement made between both parents before the divorce stating that the marriage is over and agreeing on such things as where the children should live, how much child support must be paid, and how to divide up the marital assets, such as cars and the home.

no-fault divorce—The law in some states that ends a marriage without one of the parties having to accuse the other of doing something wrong. Some states still require grounds for divorce, such as abandonment.

spouse—A legally married husband or wife.

stepbrothers and stepsisters—The children of the stepparent.

stepparent—Someone who marries after a parent has divorced.

stipulations—These are the judge-signed agreements between parents on how to divide the property and how the visitation or custody schedule is to run.

uncontested divorce—A divorce where both parents agree on all terms of the divorce and both want the marriage to end.

visitation—Times set aside for children to visit the non-custodial parent. A visitation schedule will usually include alternate weekends, some weekdays, holidays, birthdays, summer vacations, and school vacations.

Further Reading

Aydt, Rachel. *Why Me?: A Teen Guide to Divorce and Your Feelings.* New York: Rosen Publishing Group, 2000.

Block, Joel D., and Susan S. Bartell. *Stepliving for Teens: Getting Along with Stepparents, Parents and Siblings.* New York: Price Stern Sloan, 2001.

Bode, Janet, and Stan Mack. *For Better, For Worse: A Guide to Surviving Divorce for Preteens and Their Families.* New York: Simon & Schuster Books for Young Readers, 2001.

Calhoun, Florence. *No Easy Answers: A Teen Guide to Why Divorce Happens.* New York: Rosen Publishing Group, 2000.

Isler, Claudia. *Caught in the Middle: A Teen Guide to Custody.* New York: Rosen Publishing Group, 2000.

Kuehn, Eileen, and Roderick W. Franks. *Divorce: Finding a Place.* Mankato, Minn.: LifeMatters, 2001.

MacGregor, Cynthia. *The Divorce Helpbook for Kids.* Atascadero, Calif.: Impact Publishers, 2001.

Winchester, Kent, and Roberta Beyer. *What in the World Do You Do When Your Parents Divorce.* Minneapolis, Minn.: Free Spirit Publishing, 2001.

Internet Addresses

Kids' Turn
<http://www.kidsturn.org/kids/aboutus.htm>

Kids Count Program
<http://www.kidscountprogram.org>

TeensHealth
<http://www.teenshealth.org/teen/your_mind/>

Index